Behold the Lamb:

A Haggadah for Believers in Yeshua

Written and compiled by Sarah Hawkes Valente
©2024 Whatever is Lovely Publications LLC
All rights reserved.

Table of Contents

Author's Note:

We're honored that you chose to remember the Passover with us!

In this version of the *Haggadah* (which means "the telling" in Hebrew) you will see the capital letters YHVH used for the name of God. These are the letters behind every capitalized use of the word LORD in Scripture. This is the name of our God!

God has many titles: Healer, Savior, Redeemer, Shepherd, Father... But His Name is found in the mystery of these four Hebrew letters: Yod, Hey, Vav, Hey. Unfortunately for us today, the pronunciation of these letters is somewhat of a mystery. Please feel free to pronounce them as Yahwey, Yehovah, or simply as God or the LORD—whatever you are used to.

In this Haggadah, I've also used the Hebrew name for our Savior: *Yeshua*. The Hebrew word Yeshua best translates as Savior or Salvation. Consider the meaning of His mighty name as we remember the ancient Israelites' rescue from Egypt as well as our rescue from sin.

Tonight we will work our way together through the symbolic seder plate. The seder service revolves around 4 cups (pour lightly!). Dinner will be served after the 4th cup. Be sure to save some room!

Remember, normal table manners are unnecessary during a seder! Feel free to relax and lean back in your chair or lean forward with your elbows on the table. We are reclining at table tonight! Also, do not eat or drink anything until specifically directed to do so. That way we can all enjoy this experience together.

Chag Pesach sameach! Happy Passover!

Sarah Hawkes Valente

Leader: Most of us who gather today were born as gentiles. Still, we gather gratefully as those who Scripture says passed through the sea along with Moses, Miriam, and Aaron (1 Corinthians 10:1). We trust the Scriptures are true, and we believe that Israel's family is our family—their heritage, our heritage—their sorrow, our sorrow—their hope, our hope. As strangers and sojourners who are allowed the privilege through Yeshua of becoming part of His cherished family, we remember the Passover. We remember it in accordance with the commandment, "both to the native-born and to the foreigner living among you" (Exodus 12:49). We believe that we are the representation of the Temple on Earth today, and we long for the day when we can keep the Feast in the New Jerusalem—the Kingdom that is coming! As we celebrate the first exodus with all of Israel, we also remember the greater exodus from sin provided by the perfect Passover Lamb, Yeshua our Messiah. We pray that all of Israel will come to see Him for who He is.

Reader 1: Psalms 120 - 134 were sung by the Israelites on their way to Jerusalem at Feast times. Because of this, they are called the Psalms of Ascent. Psalm by Psalm, they grew closer to the Father's House and to the Presence of the God of Abraham, Isaac, and Jacob. As we read these Psalms together, may we also journey all the way into the center of His glorious presence. May we go from a place of weeping to a place of joy.

Reader 2: Psalm 120: In my distress I cried to YHVH, and He heard me. Deliver my soul, O YHVH, from lying lips and from a deceitful tongue. What will be given to you, or what will be done to you, you false tongue? Sharp arrows of the mighty, with coals of juniper. Woe is me, that I live in Meshech, that I dwell among the tents of Kedar! My soul has long dwelt with him who hates peace. I am for peace, but when I speak, they are for war.

Reader 3: Psalm 121: I will lift up my eyes to the hills. Where does my help come from? My help comes from YHVH, who made Heaven and Earth. He will not allow your foot to be moved; He who keeps you will not slumber. Behold, He who keeps Israel will neither slumber nor sleep. YHVH is your keeper; YHVH is your shade on your right hand. The sun will not strike you by day, nor the moon by night. YHVH will preserve you from all evil; He will preserve your soul. YHVH will preserve your going out and your coming in from this time forth, and even forevermore.

Reader 4: The meal we are preparing to eat is called a *Pesach* or Passover Seder. The word *seder* means "the order of service." This booklet we are using to guide us through this seder is called a *haggadah*. The word haggadah means "the telling." This comes from Exodus 13:8: "You will answer your son in that day, saying, 'It is because of what

YHVH did for me when I came out of Egypt.'" This special haggadah celebrates ancient Israel's freedom from slavery in Egypt as well as our freedom from slavery to sin which was made possible by the blood of the Lamb.

Reader 5: During the Babylonian exile, Passover was transformed from a Temple-centered festival to one centered in the home. Though the modern seder structure was not fully formed until several centuries after the Babylonian exile, the home seder was already an established practice by the time of Yeshua. The home seder as we know it today is meant to retell the Exodus story and to answer questions posed by children.

Leader: In the days before Passover, I have searched my house and removed all leavened items. The instruction to do so is found in Exodus 12:19-20: "For seven days no yeast is to be found in your houses. Indeed, whoever eats anything with yeast in it during this time will be cut off from the congregation of Israel, whether he is a foreigner or one born in the land. You will eat nothing leavened. In all your dwellings, you will eat unleavened bread."

Reader 6: As followers of Yeshua, we know that the New Testament Scriptures often use leaven as a symbol of sin. 1 Corinthians 5:6-8 reads: "Don't you know that a little leaven leavens the whole lump? Purge out the old leaven, that you may be a new lump, as you are unleavened. For indeed, Messiah, our Passover, was sacrificed for us. Therefore let us keep the feast, not with old leaven, nor with the leaven of malice and wickedness, but with the unleavened bread of sincerity and truth."

Leader: Because Yeshua brings a fuller, deeper meaning to all that came before Him, we, as His followers, should especially ask Him to search us for the leaven of sin that hides in our hearts and minds. Before we continue, let's take a moment to bow before Him and ask Him to search us.

Reader 7: Psalm 122: I was glad when they said to me, "Let's go to YHVH's house." Our feet are standing within your gates, Jerusalem. Jerusalem, that is built as a city that is compact together: Where the tribes go up, even YHVH's tribes, according to an ordinance for Israel, to give thanks to YHVH's name. For there are set thrones for judgment, the thrones of David's house. Pray for the peace of Jerusalem. Those who love you will prosper. Peace be within your walls, and prosperity within your palaces. For my brothers' and companions' sakes, I will now say, "Peace be within you." For YHVH's house, the house of our God, I will seek your good.

Reader 8: Psalm 123: To You I lift up my eyes, You who sit in the heavens. Behold, as the eyes of servants look to the hand of their master, as the eyes of a maid to the hand of her mistress, so our eyes look to YHVH, our God, until He has mercy on us. Have mercy on us, YHVH, have mercy on us, for we have endured much contempt. Our soul is exceedingly filled with the scoffing of those who are at ease, with the contempt of the proud.

Reader 9: Exodus 12:14, 24-27a: And this day will be a memorial for you, and you will keep it as a feast to YHVH; throughout your generations you will keep it a feast by an ordinance forever. You will observe this thing for an ordinance to you and to your sons forever. It will happen when you come to the land which YHVH will give you, as He has promised, that you will keep this service. It will happen when your children ask you, "What do you mean by this service?" Then you will say, "It is the sacrifice of YHVH's Passover, who passed over the houses of the children of Israel in Egypt when he struck the Egyptians and delivered our houses."

Reader 10: Exodus 13:3: And Moses said to the people, "Remember this day in which you came out from Egypt, out of the house of bondage; for by strength of hand YHVH brought you out from this place: no leavened bread will be eaten."

Lighting of the Candles

All: Blessed are You, YHVH our God, King of the Universe, Who sanctified us with His commandments and commanded us to be a light unto the nations and Who gave to us Yeshua, the Light of the World and our Passover Lamb. Amen. **(light the candles.)**

The Four Cups

Reader 11: As we read through this haggadah, we will pour the fruit of the vine into our cups four times. These four cups stand for the four "I wills" recorded in Exodus 6:6-8: Therefore, tell the Israelites: "I am YHVH, and **I will bring you out** from under the burdens of the Egyptians, and **I will deliver you** from their bondage. **I will redeem you** with an outstretched arm and with great judgments. **I will take you to myself for a people and be to you a God.** You will know that I am YHVH your God who brings you out from under the burdens of the Egyptians."

1. The Cup of Sanctification: "I will bring you out from under the burdens of the Egyptians."

2. The Cup of Deliverance: "I will deliver you from their bondage."

3. The Cup of Redemption: "I will redeem you with an outstretched arm."

4. The Cup of Praise and Restoration: "I will take you as my own people."

Reader 12: Psalm 124: "If it had not been YHVH who was on our side," let Israel now say; "If it had not been YHVH who was on our side when men rose up against us, then they would have swallowed us alive when their wrath was kindled against us. Then the waters would have overwhelmed us; the stream would have gone over our soul. The proud waters would have gone over our soul." Blessed be YHVH, who has not given us as a prey to their teeth. Our soul has escaped like a bird out of the fowler's snare. The snare is broken, and we have escaped. Our help is in YHVH's name, who made Heaven and Earth.

Reader 1: Psalm 125: Those who trust in YHVH are as Mount Zion, which can't be moved, but remains forever. As the mountains surround Jerusalem, so YHVH surrounds his people from this time forward and forevermore. For the scepter of wickedness won't remain over the allotment of the righteous, so that the righteous won't use their hands to do evil. Do good, YHVH, to those who are good, to those who are upright in their hearts. But as for those who turn away to their crooked ways, YHVH will lead them away with the workers of iniquity. Peace be on Israel.

The First Cup - Kos Kidush - The Cup of Sanctification

Reader 2: The first cup we will drink is called *Kiddush*. Kiddush is Hebrew for sanctification. The act of sanctification is an act of separation. YHVH said that He would bring the Israelites out (or separate them) from the burdens of the Egyptians—the burdens of their slavery and the burdens of their gods.

Reader 3: To be sanctified is to be set apart for His use. We are setting apart this time to bring honor to YHVH. Remember how He set apart His people in Egypt, how He set them apart in the wilderness, and how He continues to desire a set apart people who are strangers to this world.

Reader 4: YHVH redeemed us from sin and set us apart for His use when we accepted Yeshua as our Messiah.

YHVH, King of Israel, please teach us how to be strangers to the world and friends to You. Help us to desire sanctification. Help us to see the standards of the world as burdens and Your ways as freedom. Help us to see sin as the enslaver and You as the One who sets us free to walk in blessing.

Blessing of the Fruit of the Vine

(Pour the first cup.)

All: Blessed are You, YHVH our God, King of the universe, Who creates the fruit of the vine. Amen.

(Drink all of the first cup.)

Reader 5: Psalm 126: When YHVH brought back those who returned to Zion, we were like those who dream. Then our mouth was filled with laughter and our tongue with singing. Then they said among the nations, "YHVH has done great things for them." YHVH has done great things for us! We are glad. Restore our fortunes again, YHVH, like the streams in the Negev. Those who sow in tears will reap in joy. He who goes out weeping, carrying seed for sowing, will certainly come again with joy, carrying his sheaves.

Washing of Hands and Feet

Leader: YHVH commanded Aaron to wash his hands and feet before approaching the altar. We wash our hands now as a token of our desire to live clean lives of acceptable service to Him.

(Using the pitcher and bowl provided, pour water over the hands of the person on your left.)

We also wash each other's feet as a reminder that before His death Yeshua humbled Himself by washing the feet of His disciples. (Give optional foot-washing instructions.)

Reader 6: John 13:5, 12-16: Then He poured water into the basin and began to wash the disciples' feet and wipe them with the towel that was wrapped around Him. So when He had washed their feet, put his outer garment back on, and sat down again,

He said to them, "Do you know what I have done to you? You call me, 'Teacher' and 'Lord.' You say so correctly, for so I am. If I then, the Lord and the Teacher, have washed your feet, you also ought to wash one another's feet. For I have given you an example, that you should also do as I have done to you. Most certainly I tell you, a servant is not greater than his lord, neither is one who is sent greater than he who sent him.

Karpas - Dipping of the Parsley

Leader: This parsley represents the hyssop that the Israelites used to place the blood upon the doorframes of their houses—marking their thresholds for YHVH.

Parsley also embodies the vitality and new life of springtime. This salt water symbolizes the tears shed in Egypt because life there was full of pain and suffering. Take a sprig of parsley and dip it into the salt water, remembering that life is sometimes immersed in tears. **(Dip the parsley in salt water.)**

Blessing of the Karpas

All: Blessed are You, YHVH our God, King of the universe, Who creates the fruit of the earth. Amen. **(Eat the parsley.)**

Yachutz - Breaking of the Middle Matzah

Leader: Though there are three sections, this matzah found in a special covering is called a Unity (for Abraham, Isaac, and Jacob). In Hebrew, the middle of something represents the heart. Traditionally, the middle piece of matzah is removed, broken in half, and then one half is hidden away in a linen napkin. We know that Isaac was a picture of the Messiah, and in breaking the middle matzah, we remember the suffering of our Messiah, Yeshua. (Break the middle matzah; wrap the larger piece in the napkin.)

(Hold up wrapped portion.) We call this bread wrapped in linen the *afikomen*, a Greek word meaning "that which comes after," such as the dessert of a meal. Close your eyes as I hide the afikomen to represent Yeshua being "hidden" in the tomb for three days and three nights. After this special dinner, the children may look for it. There might be a prize for the finder!

Reader 7: Psalm 127: Unless YHVH builds the house, they labor in vain who build it. Unless YHVH watches over the city, the watchman stays awake in vain. It is in vain for you to rise up early, to stay up late, eating the bread of toil, for He gives sleep to His loved ones. Behold, children are a heritage of YHVH. The fruit of the womb is His reward. As arrows in the hand of a mighty man, so are the children of one's youth. Happy is the man who has his quiver full of them. They won't be shamed; they will speak with their enemies in the gate.

Reader 8: Psalm 128: Blessed is everyone who fears YHVH, who walks in His ways. For you will eat the labor of your hands. You will be happy, and it will be well with you. Your wife will be as a fruitful vine in the innermost parts of your house; your children will be like olive plants around your table. These are the blessings for the man who fears YHVH. May YHVH bless you out of Zion, and may you see the good of Jerusalem all the days of your life. Yes, may you see your children's children. Peace be upon Israel.

Ma-Nishtanah - The Four Questions

Child Reader(s):

"Why is this night different from all other nights?"

"On all other nights, we eat either leavened or unleavened bread; why on this night do we eat only matzah which is unleavened bread?"

"On all other nights, we eat vegetables and herbs of all kinds; why on this night do we eat only bitter herbs?"

"On all other nights, we never think of dipping herbs in water or in anything else; why on this night do we dip the parsley in salt water and the bitter herbs in charoset?"

"On all other nights, we eat either sitting upright or reclining. Why on this night do we recline?"

Leader: I am glad you asked these questions! This night is different from all other nights, because on this night we celebrate the going forth of the Israelites from slavery into freedom.

Why do we eat only matzah tonight? When Pharaoh let the Israelites go from Egypt, they were forced to flee quickly. They had no time to bake their bread and could not wait for the yeast to make it rise.

Why do we eat bitter herbs tonight? Because the Israelites were slaves in Egypt, and their lives were made very bitter.

12

Why do we dip the herbs in salt water and charoset tonight? We dip the parsley in salt water because it reminds us that life for the Israelites as slaves in Egypt was full of sorrow. We dip the bitter herbs in sweet charoset to remind us that the Israelites were able to withstand their slavery because of the hope of freedom.

Why do we recline at the table? Because long ago, reclining during mealtime was a sign of a free man. Since the Israelites were freed on this night, we recline at the table.

Reader 9: Psalm 129: "Many times they have afflicted me from my youth." May Israel now say: "Many times they have afflicted me from my youth, yet they have not prevailed against me. The plowers plowed upon my back; they made their furrows long. YHVH is righteous; He has cut me from the cords of the wicked."

Let all who hate Zion be confused and turned back. Let them be like the grass on the roof that withers before it grows so the reaper cannot fill his hands and the gatherer cannot bind sheaves. May those who pass by not say to them, "The blessing of YHVH be upon you," or "We bless you in the name of YHVH."

The Second Cup - Kos Matzah - The Cup of Deliverance

(Pour the second cup.)

Reader 10: YHVH raised up Moses to deliver the Israelites from bondage. God told Moses to go to Pharaoh and demand that the children of Israel be released so that they could worship YHVH His way. YHVH also told Moses that Pharaoh would not be willing to release them: "But I know that the king of Egypt will not let you go unless a mighty hand compels him. So I will stretch out My hand and strike the Egyptians with all the wonders that I will perform among them. After that, he will let you go" (Exodus 3:19-20). God struck the Egyptians with terrible plagues, and they suffered greatly. It was through these acts that He delivered His people.

Leader: Each Passover cup is a full cup of joy except for this second cup, because God teaches us never to rejoice over the fate of our enemies. For this reason, the second cup must be reduced.

Take a piece of matzah and place it in front of you. To reduce this second cup, dip your finger into your cup to remove one drop for each plague. Splash this drop onto a piece of matzah that will not be eaten.

All: Blood! **(dip and splash)** Frogs! **(dip and splash)** Gnats! **(dip and splash)** Flies! **(dip and splash)** Pestilence! **(dip and splash)** Boils! **(dip and splash)** Hail! **(dip and splash)** Locusts! **(dip and splash)** Darkness! **(dip and splash)** Slaying of the firstborn! **(dip and splash)**

Reader 11: Truly, we can say Hallelujah for the great redemption that God has accomplished for us, redemption at a terrible price: in Egypt, the death of the first-born; for us, redemption from sin through the death of God's Son.

All: "For God so loved the world, that He gave His only begotten Son, that whoever believes in Him shall not perish, but have eternal life" (John 3:16).

Blessing of the Fruit of the Vine

All: Blessed are You, YHVH our God, King of the universe, Who creates the fruit of the vine. Amen.

(Drink all of the second cup.)

The Passover Lamb

Reader 12: We can clearly see the Messiah's fulfillment (He brings more meaning) of Passover. These are the qualifications that a Passover lamb must meet (from Exodus 12) and the connections to our Messiah:

1. It was a male of the first year. Yeshua was the firstborn.

2. It was set aside for four days from the tenth of Nisan. Yeshua publicly entered Jerusalem on this same day.

3. It had no blemish. Yeshua was without sin.

4. The death penalty was imposed as soon as the lamb was chosen. Yeshua was chosen from the foundation of the world to take our penalty.

5. No bone was broken in the lamb. There were no bones broken in Yeshua.

6. The entirety of the lamb had to be consumed in one night. Yeshua was crucified and died in one night.

7. Salvation for the Israelites came by applying the blood of the lamb to their door-posts. The blood of Yeshua is salvation for all who receive it.

Reader 1: Isaiah 53:6-7 also has this to say about the Messiah, "We like sheep have gone astray; we have each turned to our own way; YHVH has laid on Him the sin of us all. He was oppressed, and He was afflicted, yet He did not open His mouth: He was brought as a lamb to the slaughter, and as a sheep before its shearers is silent, so He didn't open His mouth."

"John saw Yeshua coming to him and said, 'Behold the Lamb of God who takes away the sin of the world'" (John 1:29).

All: "Worthy is the Lamb having been slain to receive power and riches and wisdom, and strength and respect and esteem and blessing!" (Revelation 5:12).

The Seder Plate

Yachatz Matzah

Reader 2: We eat matzah during this feast to remind us that there was not enough time for the Israelites' dough to rise when YHVH redeemed them. When He said it was time to go, it was time to go quickly! "They baked unleavened cakes of the dough they brought out of Egypt. It wasn't leavened because they were forced out of Egypt and couldn't wait, and they had not prepared any food for themselves" (Exodus 12:39).

Reader 3: The matzah is unleavened, pierced, and striped—unleavened because it is to be without contamination (or sin). For those of us who are Believers in Messiah, its pierced and striped appearance points to Him. He, being without sin, was pierced and striped.

Isaiah 53:5: "But He was pierced for our transgressions; He was crushed for our wrong-doings. The punishment for our peace was laid upon Him, and by His stripes we are healed."

Reader 4: "And I will pour out on the house of David, and on the inhabitants of Jerusalem, the spirit of grace and of pleading: and they will look on Me whom they have pierced, and they will mourn for Him as one mourns for his only child, and they will weep for Him as one weeps for his firstborn" Zechariah 12:10.

Blessing of the Matzah

All: Blessed are You, YHVH our God, King of the Universe, Who brings forth bread from the earth. Amen. Blessed are You, YHVH our God, King of the Universe, Who sanctified us with His commandments and commanded us to eat the matzah. Amen. **(Eat a small piece of matzah.)**

Maror

Reader 5: This bitter herb (horseradish) symbolizes the bitterness of slavery. Exodus 1:13-14: "The Egyptians ruthlessly made the children of Israel serve, and they made their lives bitter with hard work in mortar and in brick and in all kinds of work in the field—in all their work which they ruthlessly made them do." We are reminded of the sorrow, suffering, and persecution of His people both then and today. We are also reminded of the bitterness of our sins and the suffering Yeshua had to endure because of them.

Blessing of the Maror

All: Blessed are You, YHVH our God, King of the Universe, Who sanctified us with His commandments and commanded us to eat the maror. Amen. **(Take a small piece of matzah and dip it into the maror before eating.)**

Charoset

Reader 6: Once again, we will eat the bitter herbs with the matzah, but this time we will add sweet charoset (apples and raisins). The charoset symbolizes the mortar that the Israelites used in brick making during their slavery. It is a sweet mixture, however, to remind us of the hope of freedom. At this time, let us also remember that Yeshua, the Bread of Life, holds our hope of freedom in His promise of the resurrection (1 Corinthians 15:20-22, 41-45). As He told us in John 6:50-51: "This is the bread that comes down from Heaven, that anyone who eats of it will not die. I am the living bread that came down from Heaven. If anyone eats of this bread, they will live forever; the bread that I will give is my flesh, which I will give for the life of the world."

(Take a small piece of matzah and dip it in maror and charoset.)

Blessing of the Bread of Heaven and the Hope of Eternal Life

All: Blessed are You, YHVH our God, King of the Universe, Who brings forth the True Bread from Heaven which frees us from slavery to sin and flesh and gives us the hope of eternal life. Amen. **(Eat the matzah with maror and charoset.)**

Zayit – Olives

Reader 7: There are two types of olives on our seder plate. These represent the two houses: the House of Judah which in large part has not yet recognized Yeshua as the Messiah, and the House of Israel which was scattered among the nations as lost sheep without a shepherd. Our hope and prayer is that YHVH will reunite all of Israel soon. Jeremiah 31:31-34 reads: "The days are coming," declares YHVH, "when I will make a new covenant with the people of Israel and with the people of Judah. It will not be like the covenant I made with their ancestors when I took them by the hand to lead them out of Egypt, because they broke my covenant, though I was a husband to them," declares YHVH. "This is the covenant I will make with the people of Israel after that time," declares YHVH. "I will put my law in their minds and write it on their hearts. I will be their God, and they will be my people. No longer will they teach their neighbor, or say to one another, 'Know YHVH,' because they will all know me, from the least of them to the greatest," declares YHVH. "For I will forgive their wickedness and will remember their sins no more."

Hallelujah!

Olives are also representative of peace and security. Let us continually pray for the peace of Jerusalem. Amen. **(Eat the olives.)**

Dayenu

Leader: We do not rejoice over the fate of our enemies, but we should never let ourselves forget the magnitude of God's salvation and His miraculous actions toward us. With grateful hearts and a healthy fear of YHVH, we say, "*Dayenu*, it would have been enough." We remember the many great acts that God has done on behalf of His people. The Dayenu is an important part of a traditional Jewish seder. This one includes some additional lines.

Reader 8: Did you know that you are one of Abraham's children? God's family started with a physical seed and a genetic line of promise, but it didn't stop there! Before we begin the Dayenu, let's review how we fit into the big picture.

"And so Abraham believed God, and it was counted to him for righteousness. In the same way, those who are of faith, the same are the children of Abraham. And scripture, foreseeing that God would justify the gentiles through faith, preached the gospel to Abraham, saying, 'In you will all nations be blessed.' So then they who are of faith are blessed with Abraham, who believed" (Galatians 3:6-9).

Worship Leader: We've known we were Father Abraham's children since we were kids in Sunday school. Here's a little reminder! (Lead one or more verses of Father Abraham.

Father Abraham

Right arm! Father
Left arm!
Right leg!
Left leg!
Turn around!
Sit down!

Leader: If He had promised the land to Abraham but had not renewed the promise to Isaac and Jacob

All: Dayenu, it would have been enough!

Leader: If He had renewed the promise to Isaac and Jacob but had not sent us to Egypt to save our lives

All: Dayenu, it would have been enough!

Leader: If He had sent us to Egypt to save our lives but had not caused us to thrive there

All: Dayenu, it would have been enough!

Leader: If He had caused us to thrive in Egypt but had not brought us out

All: Dayenu, it would have been enough!

Leader: If He had brought us out from the Egyptians but had not carried out judgments against them

All: Dayenu, it would have been enough!

Leader: If He had carried out judgments against them but had not destroyed their idols

All: Dayenu, it would have been enough!

Leader: If He had destroyed their idols but had not given us their wealth

All: Dayenu, it would have been enough!

Leader: If He had given us their wealth but had not split the sea for us

All: Dayenu, it would have been enough!

Leader: If He had split the sea for us but had not taken us through it on dry land

All: Dayenu, it would have been enough!

Leader: If He had taken us through the sea on dry land but had not drowned our oppressors in it

All: Dayenu, it would have been enough!

Leader: If He had drowned our oppressors in the sea but had not supplied our needs in the desert for forty years

All: Dayenu, it would have been enough!

Leader: If He had supplied our needs in the desert for forty years but had not fed us the manna

All: Dayenu, it would have been enough!

Leader: If He had fed us the manna but had not given us the Sabbath

All: Dayenu, it would have been enough!

Leader: If He had given us the Sabbath but had not brought us before Mount Sinai

All: Dayenu, it would have been enough!

Leader: If He had brought us before Mount Sinai but had not given us the Torah

All: Dayenu, it would have been enough!

Leader: If He had given us the Torah but had not brought us into the Promised Land

All: Dayenu, it would have been enough!

Leader: If He had brought us into the Promised Land but had not built for us the Holy Temple

All: Dayenu, it would have been enough!

Leader: If He had built for us the Holy Temple but had not preserved Judah

All: Dayenu, it would have been enough!

Leader: If He had preserved Judah but had not sent His Son to be born as the Lion of the Tribe of Judah

All: Dayenu, it would have been enough!

Leader: If He had sent His Son to be born as the Lion of the Tribe of Judah but had not also sent Him as the perfect Passover Lamb

All: Dayenu, it would have been enough!

Leader: If He had sent His Son as the perfect Passover Lamb but had not given Him for the whole world

All: Dayenu, it would have been enough!

Leader: If He had given Him for the whole world but had not raised Him from the dead to give us hope of resurrection

All: Dayenu, it would have been enough!

Leader: If Yeshua had been raised from the dead to give us hope of resurrection but had not returned to the Father to prepare a place for us

All: Dayenu, it would have been enough!

Leader: If Yeshua had returned to the Father to prepare a place for us but had not sent the Holy Spirit to comfort and teach us

All: Dayenu, it would have been enough!

Reader 9: When Moses led the people through on dry ground where the sea had been the day before, the people sang and rejoiced. We should always remember that just because a sea blocks our way today, that does not mean it will be there in the morning! Our spiritual ancestors walked through the sea, and we've crossed from death to life in Messiah.

Worship Leader: (Lead one or more verses of I Will Sing unto Yahweh.)

I Will Sing unto Yahweh

1. I will sing unto Yahweh for He has triumphed gloriously,
The horse and rider thrown into the sea.

I will sing unto Yahweh for He has triumphed gloriously,
Our mighty Lord has crushed the enemy.

Chorus:

Yahweh, my God, my strength, my song, has now become my victory.

Yahweh, my God, my strength, my song, has now become my victory.

Yahweh is God and I will praise Him, my father's God and I will exalt Him.

Yahweh is God and I will praise Him, our father's God and I will exalt Him!

2. I will sing unto Yahweh for He has triumphed gloriously,
And all who hear of His great power will fear.

I will sing unto Yahweh for He has triumphed gloriously,
Yahweh will bring His people forth from here.

3. I will sing unto Yahweh for He has triumphed gloriously,
He'll lead us to the land that is our home.

I will sing unto Yahweh for He has triumphed gloriously,
He's bought us and He's going to take us home.

The Third Cup - Kos HaGeulah - The Cup of Redemption

(Pour the third cup.)

Reader 10: The fruit of the vine we drink tonight represents the blood of the Passover lamb. The blood of the lamb was spilled and applied to the doorposts of the houses of the Israelites to allow for their salvation. To us, this also brings to mind the cup that Yeshua was holding in Matthew 26:27-29: "And He took the cup, gave thanks, and gave it to them, saying, 'Drink from it, all of you. This is my blood of the covenant, which is shed for many for forgiveness of sins. But I tell you, I will not drink of this fruit of the vine until that day when I drink it new with you in my Father's kingdom."

Yeshua did not drink from this cup because it was representative of redemption. It would not be long after His refusal to drink that He would become our Redemption.

Blessing of the Fruit of the Vine

All: Blessed are You, YHVH our God, King of the universe, Who creates the fruit of the vine. Amen.

(Drink all of the third cup.)

The Fourth Cup - Kos HaShir - The Cup of Praise

Reader 11: Psalm 130: Out of the depths I have cried to you, YHVH. YHVH, hear my voice: let Your ears be attentive to my cries. If you, YHVH, kept track of sins, who could stand? But there is forgiveness with You, so that You may be feared. I wait for YHVH; my soul waits, and in His word do I hope. My soul waits for the Lord more than they that watch for the morning: I say, more than they that watch for the morning. Let Israel hope in YHVH; for with YHVH there is mercy, and with Him is complete redemption. He will redeem Israel from all their sins.

Reader 12: Psalm 131: YHVH, my heart is not haughty nor my eyes proud, neither do I concern myself with important matters or things too wonderful for me. Surely I have behaved and quieted myself like a weaned child with his mother: like a weaned child my soul is content. Let Israel hope in YHVH from now and forever.

Reader 1: Psalm 132: YHVH, remember David and all his afflictions. He swore to YHVH and vowed unto the mighty God of Jacob, "I will not go into my house or go to my bed; I will not give sleep to my eyes or rest to my eyelids until I find a place for YHVH, a House for the mighty God of Jacob." We heard of it at Ephratah: we found it in the fields of the wood: "We will go into His tabernacle; we will worship at His footstool. Arise, YHVH, into Your rest—You, and the ark of Your strength. Let Your priests be clothed with righteousness, and let Your saints shout for joy." For Your servant David's sake, do not turn away the face of Your anointed.

Reader 2: Psalm 132 cont.: YHVH swore to David, and He will not turn from His word, "One of your descendants I will place on your throne. If your children keep My covenant and My laws that I will teach them, their children will sit on your throne forever." For YHVH has chosen Zion; He has desired it for His habitation: "This is My rest forever: here will I dwell, for I have desired it. I will abundantly bless her provision; I will satisfy her poor with bread. I will clothe her priests with salvation and her saints will shout for joy. I will make the horn of David bud and ordain a lamp for My anointed. I will clothe His enemies with shame, but I will adorn His head with a radiant crown."

Reader 3: Psalm 133: Behold, how good and how pleasant it is for God's people to dwell together in unity! It is like precious oil poured on the head and running down the beard, even Aaron's beard, down to the skirt of his robe. It is as the dew of Hermon and as the dew on the mountains of Zion. For there the Lord commanded the blessing, even life forevermore.

Reader 4: Psalm 134: Bless YHVH, all you servants of YHVH who minister by night in the house of YHVH. Lift up your hands in the sanctuary, and bless YHVH. May YHVH who made Heaven and Earth bless you from Zion.

Reader 5: We will now pour the fourth cup: the Cup of Praise and Restoration. This cup reminds us to praise Him for the redemption and salvation that He so graciously offers us. Romans 6:23: "For the wages of sin is death, but the favorable gift of God is everlasting life in Messiah Yeshua our Master." **(Pour the fourth cup.)**

Reader 6: This cup is also a reminder for us to look ahead to His return.

1 Thessalonians 4:16-18: "For the Lord Himself will come down from Heaven, with a loud command, with the voice of the archangel and with the trumpet call of God, and the dead in Christ will rise first. After that, we who are still alive and are left will be caught up together with them in the clouds to meet the Lord in the air. And so we will be with the Lord forever. Therefore encourage one another with these words."

Reader 7: As we drink this last cup, we pray for Your Truth to be revealed to Your people, salvation for all, restoration of Your Kingdom, and the return of our Messiah, Yeshua.

Blessing of the Fruit of the Vine

All: I will lift up the cup of salvation and call upon the Name of YHVH.

All: Blessed are You, YHVH our God, King of the universe, Who creates the fruit of the vine. Amen.

(Drink all of the fourth cup.)

Leader: There is another cup mentioned in Scripture: the cup of God's wrath that Jeremiah was to deliver to the nations (Jeremiah 25:15); "the fruit of the vine of God's fury…poured full strength into the cup of His wrath" (Revelation 14:10); the "cup of the wrath of the Almighty" (Job 21:20); the "cup of His wrath…that makes people stagger" (Isaiah 51:17, 22; Psalm 75:8).

This is the cup that sat before Yeshua on the night before His death. He pleaded with God, asking His Father not to make Him drink of this terrible cup. The divine wrath of God was to be poured out from this cup as the judgment for sin resulting in physical suffering and death, mental torment and agony over sin and the resulting abandonment by the Father, and the fierce anger and fury of God being poured out on the One compelled to drink it. In the end, Yeshua willingly drank every drop of this cup for us. Look at your empty cup, and praise Him for His willing sacrifice.

Shulchan Orech – Prepared Table

Blessing over the Meal

All: Hear O Israel, YHVH our God, YHVH is One. Blessed is the name of His glorious kingdom forever. And you shall love YHVH your God with all your heart, with all your soul, and with all your might. These words, which I command you this day, shall be upon your heart. You shall teach them diligently to your children. You shall speak of them when you sit in your house, when you walk by the way, when you lie down, and when you rise up. You shall bind them as a sign upon your hand and as frontlets between your eyes. And you shall write them on the doorposts of your house and on your gates. And you shall love your neighbor as yourself.

Leader: Blessed are You, YHVH our God, King of the universe, Who has commanded that we remember the Feasts of Passover and Unleavened Bread. Thank You for the redemption and salvation You sent—first in Egypt when You rescued Your People from bondage and second by sending Your Son, Yeshua, to redeem us from the bondage of sin and offer salvation to those who will accept Him. YHVH, God of our ancestors, may our partaking of the Passover Seder be pleasing in Your sight. May the worship of Your people always be worthy of Your acceptance. We thank You for the blessing of Your holy Feasts. Send Your Spirit to fill us as we partake of this meal. Fill our hearts and minds with Your shalom—Your peace that surpasses all understanding. Guide each of us that we may bless one another with our words and actions. Come, YHVH, and dine with us tonight. Fill us as we rest in You. Thank you for building this family and strengthening us together. Amen.

All: They tried to kill us. He delivered us. Let's eat!

Name: _____ Date: _____

Passover Crossword (The clues are in the Haggadah!)

Across
2. greater _____ from sin
6. Yeshua was the _____.
8. the mortar
11. Sixth plague
13. Yeshua was without _____.
14. _____ believed God, and it was counted to him for righteousness.
16. Represents the hyssop

17. Unity
18. Pray for the peace of _____.

Down
1. "the order of service"
3. There were no _____ broken in Yeshua.
4. "I wills"
5. The blood of the lamb was spilled and applied to the _____ of the houses of the Israelites

7. "the telling"
9. After
10. Blessed are You, YHVH our God, King of the _____
12. Believers all passed through the ____
15. It would have been enough.

Passover Word Search

```
D O O L B G E F I O T S U D R H H J A E S X D U
N U N H F Z R L N R Q G O K G M M T J K W J V A
O R E M C G G M U U I B R N O U A E S P R N I N
H A P A R S L E Y S L S J S O I Q M P Q S T T O
V W S Q Q Q D O W I Q B E J G U H L U E W S V Q
L N E U W B D V X J N S I D E S G O R F V K R U
F W V H K K F L I E S A M S G N T P Q Y X B W X
R P N I S M T I E I Q W T O H X M H G F A V F Q
C C H L Y P P M M H I I K Y G D M D E P E F L Y
H T I R P X I T M C O X S Y S F B S E B I R T N
A O M F M A V N R N Z S F D Y D F O D O E S K I
B C Q F K U N I S H O K R X K R A A T U G V X R
Y W X M T B W M Q P S I Y C E U M R T Y P B E O
T E S O R A H C Y M T S Z D V I V A K S R B F S
U S F W O A I U S T Z T E W Y J J J H N C O Q U
E K F O Z O A P N X I S H O M U L E D A E R A I
X B C O W V T K E W O N S L V P X B I D R S I Q
O L F B M K M F R W K L U Z X I Z Q O N T B S N
D G M X W O K G D H X W J I J H L G H O H J A J
U Y K A D P K L L H A G G A D A H A I N R T Z M
S V C E T C Q Q I K E C T M S P J L U J E R S O
U F E G M Z F A H G C F R Z B I P J U O E D K F
D R P K N V A F C V P N E M O K I F A Q C E M A
F Q M O W G U H P L A G U E S D B C J B M O J J
```

abraham	afikomen	blood	boils	charoset
children	darkness	exodus	flies	freedom
frogs	haggadah	hyssop	matzah	moses
parsley	plagues	questions	sea	seder
sin	staff	three	tribes	unity

Let my people go!

Passover

Host/Hostess Instructions:

This Haggadah is meant to be led by 14 people:

1 leader

12 additional readers

1 worship leader

The service is expected to take an hour and a half to two hours to complete. It's recommended to serve soup and/or appetizers before the service begins to ensure that your guests aren't distracted by hunger.

Things you'll need:

Large seder plates for each table, which include:

Two types of olives

Parsley

Horseradish

Charoset

Matzah

Small bowls of salt water

Place settings for each guest, which in addition to the standard setting include:

A glass set aside for wine/juice

A small seder plate

A Haggadah booklet

Tambourines/instruments

Candles

Candle holders

Matches

Wine/juice in carafes on each table

Special wrapping for the Unity

White linen cloth for the afikomen

Small prize

Hand-washing bowls, pitchers, and hand towels

Foot-washing tubs, pitchers, and towels

Crayons/colored pencils

Did you enjoy this Haggadah? Please let us know!

www.whatislovely.online

More resources are available:

www.whatislovely.online/passover